Riding with Destiny

Riding with Destiny

by
Jayne Lyn Stahl

The New York Quarterly Foundation, Inc.
New York, New York

NYQ Books™ is an imprint of The New York Quarterly Foundation, Inc.

The New York Quarterly Foundation, Inc.
P. O. Box 2015
Old Chelsea Station
New York, NY 10113

www.nyqbooks.org

Copyright © 2010 by Jayne Lyn Stahl

All rights reserved. No part of this book may be used or reproduced in any manner whatsoever without written permission of the author. This book is a work of fiction. Any references to historical events, real people or real locales are used fictitiously. Other names, characters, places, and incidents are products of the author's imagination, and any resemblance to actual events or locales or persons, living or dead, is entirely coincidental.

First Edition

Set in New Baskerville

Layout and Design by Raymond P. Hammond
Cover Photo: "George Washington Bridge," HDR Photo,
    ©2009 Jay Dorfman | jaydorfman.arloartists.com

Library of Congress Control Number: 2010923061

ISBN: 978-1-935520-26-9

For my father
who gave me poetry which is with me now.

Contents

under that bridge	11
riding with destiny	12
Driving	13
For a soldier	14
to be carried aboard	15
a message from jayne	16
The Crowning with Thorns	18
blind as Brooklyn	19
how it starts	21
Walt Whitman's Fly	22
no small accomplishment	25
An impulse like salt	27
in this city	28
Managing Gravity	29
On Waite Street	30
Elegy for Democracy	38
Passionata	40
When dark is put away	41
in our new skin	42
White Light for Sally	44
to live with ghosts	47
two pigeons	48
at the end of rage	49
even myths	52
for Allen	54
The Russian Prince	56
so we do the primitive	62

next door	63
Execution Day in July	64
in faust's bed	65
you walk me	66
and sing your face	67
walks large	68
heaven	69
storm clouds	70
But for the grace	71
the seasons	72
fire escapes	74
Convolutions	75
blue teeth	77
The Bubblegum Thief	78
a bird	79
interview with an angel	80
their burgundy bloom	81
hanging man	82
in translation	83
USA donuts	84
rain	86
a fist of light	87
PAST TENSE	88
courtroom chrysanthemum	89
it hurts, you say, to see	90
Prometheus	91
The Still Point	92

eating peanuts	93
Erogenous Zone	94
Playing Strip Poker with Tiresias	95
Just the Same	96
in a spirited debate	98
to dine with friends	99
Waking Up on the Wall Side	100
COMES LOVE	101
La Monde N'Existe Pas Entre Nous	102
The World Doesn't Exist Between Us	103
Once	104
In Another Life	105

Riding with Destiny

under that bridge

disabuse
yourself of
this—
it's only in
foxholes
we
dirty ourselves
urgently
quietly
waiting for
somebody else's
salvation like
a train that never
comes
it is only
in trenches
we sing
only in
the steel
gut of
morning
awake to
something
spineless
that tells us
there is daring
under that bridge
but
under that
bridge is
only flight.

riding with destiny

in a blue truck
on the back of a healthy
spoon I can taste
hot nights on your thigh still you are
a stranger as you say
when you ride
with destiny you
ride alone.
you tear out photos
from old passports   scramble
names in address books
crawl into bed
you are too close your breath
like whiskey agitates
I am saddle sore from riding
I am inside out
while you laugh
in invisible diners
how curious to have invented
you in glory
holes of hell
where like a black pearl
you empty yourself
and the only danger is
thinking there is no danger
in a blue truck
on the back of
a healthy spoon
when you ride with destiny
you ride alone.

Driving

I had a
dream I got
behind
the wheel
and
started driving.
I made it around
the world
before I
ran out of
gas.

For a soldier

"Those that I fight I do not hate.
Those that I guard I do not love."
—William Butler Yeats

I risk exile just to stand in
your skin
swim to the bottom to
find where the bottom is.
you have your
wings pressed primed like Icarus just another
downed passenger jet behind
an angry sun you are
a pawn in that other great pawn shop
history where
my grandfather's watch hangs along
with his vision of
outliving this century wider
still widening gyre forgotten
just another sentry at
the gate. you swim to the bottom to
find where the bottom is you risk
exile just to stand
in my skin.

to be carried aboard

> *"Tell me at what hour I need
> to be carried aboard."*
> —Arthur Rimbaud

they took your blood
for free
they took your blood to
sample like wine
on the ship that left without you
still wild
birds amass on your Africa where
scent of your century hides
still rooms to let
on streets of
savage inquiry.
we wait like vessels
to be carried away
in hypnotic convertibles away from
apocryphal epochs where petty
ministers take your blood and
feed it to the pigeons
where they crucify you in tribute
you dance with knives
where magnificent dawnings spew
from venomous snakes and
boys shoot crap on your sails small
wonder we've already outlived ourselves.

a message from jayne

jayne has got
her own parfum
jayne has become
human
in keeping
with custom
she sells the screams
in her pocket
rides bareback white horse a
heartbeat down the side of day-
break a talkative roadmap
the kind that curves
long industrious fingers
into the fire of
a russian dance.
I am a buffoon with balloon pants
in the time of peter the great
court jester a wax museum
on sundays.
jayne has got
her own parfum
jayne has become human
in keeping
with custom
the floor falls back on itself
like a staircase in a church where
a little white monk takes his joke seriously.
I beat some eggs
sit down to a decent meal the sun
comes down like a slap on the thigh
I wake sloppily like lazarus
explain myself a billion times
in uncensored, gratuitous notes I leave

on kitchen tables of furnished rooms.
at twenty-four I stood on stilts
to see myself at seven walked home medium
from mars.
in keeping with custom
when I wear my joan of arc outfit
even my landlord calls me joan
when I rise from the dead I forget

The Crowning with Thorns

he leaves much to be desired
at table
never finishes a sentence.
crowds come to drive nails through
the designated holes in his hands.
—a modern cross, like a disposable lighter,
is propped against an altar—
someone takes bets.
the crowd cheers as he mounts the cross
a crown quickly position'd on his skull
he takes each thorn swallows it.
he holds the crown in his right hand
it changes to a mirror.
he spits thorns into the crowd
the cross dissolves
the crowd disappears
he folds the altar
into his pocket
& is gone.

blind as Brooklyn

he stands
blind as Brooklyn
after a snowstorm
just another soldier
on an empty bus
understated as
the last ferry out of
Staten Island.
how sad to
think that life
mistakes us for a
stranger to
forget prayer hanging from
the lips of
a child as she watches
her father go off to war.
who better at
exile than I
he thinks looking
straight ahead
Cross Bronx
Expressway in
his gaze fragile as
the girl sold for
a one-way
ticket on
his last tour. still
he is
just another soldier on
a cross-town bus
wondering how to smell
only his uniform fresh from
the wash not

blood rehearsing in
a bullet nor hear
dumb pulse of hand grenade
ringing in his ears.
only a siren can betray him
now or
the eyes of one he meets in
that final moment of combat
a victim not of arms but
statistics. he thinks
sometimes life
mistakes us for strangers
searching for
his gloves
just another boxer
in the dark.

how it starts…

this is how it starts
rhapsodic—
rain pouring
on the roof
like no
tomorrow
like yesterday's thunder
old news.
this is how
it starts
paned &
painless
windows open
spineless clouds
breaking through.
what propels us
compels only quiet—
a city in search of itself
a rider that is only
half horse
this is how
without purpose
the rain urges
razor sharp
downward
a quick spiral up
towards the light.

Walt Whitman's Fly

for John Logan

*"Get the gasworks into a poem,
and you've got the smoke and smokestacks,
the mottled red and yellow tenements,
and grimy kids who curse with the pungency
of the odor of gas. You've got America, boy."*
—David Ignatow

Get the gasworks into a poem
and you've got Walt Whitman
Walt—
with the sun at your left side
and death at your right you in
the middle like a daguerreotype
I remember you
your baggy buccaneer pants
hiding saucy pirates
with real-live locomotives and steam underneath
the beat-up breath of tenements.
What a smokestack you were!
your fly that became a rose in my
hand your hips haughty & the star juice I
catch from your eyes the flaring nostrils
the quaker chin the illuminations in every line
I approach you with this poem in my hand &
a warm welcome.
Walt
I know you had a gray beard how could it be
any different? as I sit here dreaming of
some manly cloud typing up
            state requisitions
for the Maintenance Office maintenant! punching
the clock
            no body electric

your time shining on my eyelids one of
the roughs.
your flashing armpits are like
traffic lights and the
    deep crimson thrill
that comes over me when I ride
the subway convinced of
    a new religion
& you in the corner (no caboose) with
your hand on
    your right hip trans-
parent like some lonely Poe-ship you created
with decks of sailors holding other hands. I imagine your
armpits to be a Japanese rainforest your smell that
prayer the saneness of your death
my death.
I look for you over my shoulder
I look for your cheekbones behind el gray
I know you hid the gasworks somewhere
the secret of your sad orb over rooftops
curious dream of factories your modern man behind tele-
visions—'yessuh
you got the world by the rear—'
and hindsight which was foresight
I look back on you because you look'd
forward to me & there is no stone
untouch'd, Walt Whitman,
can I hold you to your promise?
will I find you on the CP Rail
on a long white train through Canada
behind those camerado Rockies?

can I sneak up behind you on th'astral plane?
will you always be behind me like the Great Spirit
on the Staten Island Ferry?
I itch for you, you crazy sun of
I unbutton your shirt & find leaves
yes! growing on your chest
I wear my Spanish cowboy hat the Shadow &
dance like a red bandana the wind my voice
wrestles prophetic with every telephone pole I can
find like a bloody angel viola joan of arc
medea sans Jason or any Jacobean forget-me-not.
cheek to cheek, Walt Whitman, I have come to build
your bridge
will you settle for my hands.

no small accomplishment

he hides his liquor
well
no small
accomplishment given
his size which is
perfect for
the foxhole where
he hides as if
dark were his
and his
alone.
the shoes he
abandons by
his bedside are
patent
leather with
soles as lonely
as discarded
oaths.
who has time for
this he thinks
surely not
one who
tosses and
turns like a swollen
boat on
a vacant pier.
who knows the hollow of
his breadth knows only
the silence of
furious engines.
he holds his
liquor well in

stolen driveways and
goes to
sleep the way
others leave for war.

An impulse like salt

I can feel you between
my thighs like
a flash of
light on
dark pavement.
I can smell your
sweat on
the palm of
my hand all that's left
an impulse
like salt on
a stunning wound
this memory
a harbor without
boats still
bearing a flash of
light.

in this city

in this city that is
not just a ghost, but
a fractured ghost
those who run on
higher octane never stop to
refuel, but proceed to
nearest terminal.
in this city hasidic fear is
palpable where
hungry nurses roll
the dice behind
hoboken moon where
death hides in a doorway grinning
another sky-
scraper drops billboards sing
net prophets hawk
laptops terror lurks in
ninety-nine cent stores like
pin-up soldiers
lullabies at ground
zero wake-up call from
spring street unrepentant as
daybreak
just another un-
documented ghost in midtown
tunnel this city,
battle-
scarred, weary,
this city
will survive.

Managing Gravity

for John Thomas

Death taps me on the shoulder this morning, and says
"we need to talk"
"indeed we do," I say, & stare him squarely in
the jaw. "What have you been doing with
yourself," I ask
"managing gravity," says he, "speaking of
which you've been avoiding me"
"averting, not avoiding," says me
"that's semantics," he says
"You see me, I see you. I'm okay with being
mortal–why can't you accept defiance—
why must you constantly stand over me while I work
you make it hard to focus."
"You'd have no work were it not for me," says he
"Who died and made you god," says me.
I move close enough to smell his
breath, and tell him he doesn't stink like Dostoyevsky said—
"You're not the hot shit you think you are. Keep your hands off
my Aunt Sally—keep your hands off
poetry—what makes you think you can mess with
poets—stay in your corner, keep out of mine." He asks
"Why do you move around so much—do you think
you can escape me?"
"As long as I have moving parts, I'm going to keep moving &
I'm not going to stop even when those parts give way."

On Waite Street

for Aram Saroyan

"The monster that had resorted to arms must be put
in chains that could not be broken. The united power of
free nations must put a stop to aggression, and the world
must be given peace."
     —Woodrow Wilson
     Address to the Senate, July 10, 1919

On Waite Street I pass an
American flag with cigarette
burns in it and think
if we can't find Jimmy Hoffa
how can we find bin Laden here on
Waite Street I think
maybe we need cliff notes so
our elected officials don't have to
bother reading an act named after patriots
why read wait until
it comes out on video—coming soon to a theatre
near you—"The Patriot Act"—up close and
personal—action thriller—watch as law enforcers get to
storm through your living
room take you downtown
and hold you without telling you why—coming soon to
a theatre near you—watch as
Miranda goes up in smoke.
only the software changes
the hard drive remains the same—battlefields just as
bloody now as they were five hundred years
ago virtual reality yet to replace rigor mortis
about the only change from cave man days
is location of the cave—hell—some are even
cable ready air conditioned
some are cellular & have internet access

but how confuse acts of patriotism with patriot act.
whoever thought the
enemy would crawl out of a cave
except maybe Plato whoever thought we would see
the day when Satan could have his own web site when uranian
irregulars replace sputnik & electronic surveillance
replaces t.v. guide we have treatments for
those who are lactose intolerant
but no treatment for
those who are liar intolerant. we live behind gates
carry guns in our glove compartments
drive vans that are larger than some third
world countries.
we pay a high price for
our dreams and an even higher one for
having them come true.
funny isn't it
in this country
how crime
pays &
poetry doesn't.

on Waite Street somebody
got their signals crossed
shattered glass lines
the street like
broken dreams
that bastard in his 4 x 4 staring
off into space his head cocked
like a rifle as I step hungrily

off the curb & miss
hit pavement while he keeps staring
straight as
an arrow or a marksman bullet or
maybe a guard on
death row waiting for
light to turn green for me
to fall wondering
if he shaves
his head wondering if
I mean more or
less than road kill if he were to run
me down would he still be
able to use the same electric razor
in the morning. his head
matches the impotent
flag he fondles on his
dashboard as he debates whether to
floor the gas yes less than a minute to
get up before he mounts me
like a wild horse in
his bronco thinking his truck is
bigger than my truck. it took me
nearly fifty years to learn what fear is—
only a deer in
the headlights can relate.
it's alright with me if
evil remains an abstraction
I don't want it living
next door. it's alright
if evil remains abstract like

terror. it's not terrorists
we need to worry about—it's deer
hunters waving their flags—stoking their
arsenals—taking aim at beauty
taking aim at all that is
delicate different—
if we're looking for
the axis of evil
we have only to look
in our own backyards.

on Waite Street a flag waves on
someone's porch it could be a swastika for
all its power no nuclear pilgrims here no bare
bottom may-
flowers no free falling monuments
only dust and
collectors of dust. no victory
only illusions of victory. hatred wears
many masks—simply put
there's no there there.

real terror hides
behind flags
there can be no terror
without ideology I think
picking myself up
Don Quixote would have loved a war
like this
he loved chasing windmills somebody ought to
tell the Don that Saddam wants to

play ball—word has it he even rented
"Dead Man Walking"—
a war to camouflage assault on
civil liberties assault on
due process human rights & the right
to be read your rights—
a war on terrorism—to wax quixotic—
how about a war on abstractions.
it seems to me
there was another guy
in the old country
named George—King George—
our forefathers came here to
escape—isn't it
funny more than 200 years
later same battle different George only this one
never met
a fact he didn't invent—this one, when he's not out
making the world safe for
democracy, is home trying to rewrite
the Constitution in ways that would make even Washington
blush—oh—the real
threat doesn't come from terrorists
it comes from legislators. founding
fathers would be pleased to know
we finally have a president
who's out making the world safe
for metaphors.

incompetence is its own reward
forget hormone replacement therapy

what about human replacement
therapy what about enhancing
the gene pool with some
common decency what about garden
variety compassion empathy and yes
hosiery that doesn't run when you
pull on it.

whose idea was it to
choose the word intelligence—when lifting the cover off
the CIA the last thing we expect to see is
intelligence—that's like finding a cockroach in
a cookbook—
alas it's often easier to use one's arms
than one's head—
solve the crisis in the Middle East
give Yasser Arafat a nose job
put him in an Armani suit
give him a haircut—better still
send him & bin Laden to the same barber—
somebody needs to tell those guys
as we get older
we learn to either embrace our roots or
dye them.

our nuclear waistline is expanding
we need weight watchers for
our army fen fen for air force metamucil for
merchant marines.

I'd like another serving of

American flag, thank you
what I like best about flags is
skin heads hate crimes neo Nazis cognitive
carcinogens—make no mistake
those who torch synagogues
would crucify Christ all over again
only this time they'd be sure his eyes
were shut.

careful—real terror lurks
behind flags—it's not ideology
it's the fervor I think on
Waite Street how
democratic
even the president gets to
hide behind a flag from time to
time what a great country
where one gets to
wave a flag and jerk off
simultaneously

what if we had a war, and nobody came.

it's not fit for a poet to
descend to the level of political discourse but to
raise political discourse to
the level of poetry.

On Waite Street
I get tired of walking out

my door & tripping
over flags I'm so bored I almost
want to clean the house I liked it better
when I thought that redneck meant
carnivore. I think corporate greed belongs on
spin cycle—and the war on
terror begins at home—I confess—
when it comes right
down to it—
I don't mind giving up my
citizenship it's my bed I worry about.
here on Waite Street
history will show intelligence is
optional with the vehicle here where
we're putting off
the revolution to watch "Scooby Doo."

Elegy for Democracy

*"For my enemy is dead
a man as divine as myself is dead."*
—Walt Whitman

We're ousting leaders left &
right parading heads of
corpses on primetime television
peddling mediocrity in
our public schools pushing crack in
our inner cities watching our
credit lines contract
while our waistlines expand we put
antifreeze in our pillows
explosives in school lunches lies where
headlines should be lies voracious as
madmen at the gates of hell—
      presidential lies
      journalist lies
       electric company lies
       insider trading lies
       intelligence lies
truth crucified by
holy Hollywood card
shark lies
sparkling teeth of Clairol commercial inter-
net lies mothers tell their children to
help them sleep lies governments tell
their people —O the tangled web
we weave.
      some verbs don't lie
like heads of state in thirty second spots
or statue of liberty waiting to be
redeemed for pepsi cans in empty supermarkets.

some verbs can't help but
lie like painless victory. O
vision of stainless steel. our forefathers victims, too, of
hypocrites on
pulpits O saviors in
our breakfast cereal   O makeshift lonely
jails   O dream of freedom stalled at
our borders   O starry nights where vowels
should be where fraud and
fear are interchangeable
lies are redeemed
dirt cheap in
crowded markets   we oust leaders
in primetime   if we're ousting
leaders left and right,
surely we must fall.

Passionata

I awake to your smell
still familiar like
sweat on swollen testicles.
I awake to a face that no longer
belongs to you but to
memory your
childhood the last word in
the mouth of
a dying man a pulse that
dares from
another dimension passion
a landscape of
lovers refracted through
frozen glass like the sound gravity makes
when it shatters passionate as
brazen ghosts
never to be silenced again.

When dark is put away—

> *"We grow accustomed to the Dark when light is put away."*
> — Emily Dickinson

We dance in the streets of
Baghdad while Saddam's sons
bloated dead barely recognizable
smile for the evening news
a final deception maybe they
knew they'd be on display maybe they knew
once light is
put away illusions shine
in the dark illusions soldiers carry
like futile seeds where is
the grace in this—war a
virile exercise like
carrying a fat corpse to
 funeral pyre—
a virile enterprise for
corporations not soldiers barely
old enough to
shave now un-
recognizable to their
mothers brothers and nations that
will quickly forget
remember only
victory as we dance through
streets of
Baghdad victory polluted as
the palace we overtake impotent as
fallen leaders plucking lice from
their hair while we fill our shopping carts with
perishables our gas tanks with
salvation myths that flow like
musty semen from mouths of whores. where is
the grace in this
that shines when dark
is put away.

in our new skin

for my father

"But this, / to accept death, even before life, so gently, / the whole of death, and not to be angry/ is past description." — Rainer Maria Rilke

"Silence is the refuge of emotion." — David Darwin Stahl

We are all growing old
in our new skin
you in your army uniform barely
twenty already smothering your poems
to survive in the thirties
fresh from the army holes in your pants
your last paycheck went for a
jaguar.
we are all growing old
in our new skin
when I was five you drove up
in a lincoln continental I climbed on chair to watch
you beam at car mother screaming how
we all sleep in one room and you with your
cars you in your boxer
shorts midnight bowl of pecan ice cream
your passion the horses. you must believe
to gamble.
when I wandered off to
be alone you understood and when I ran across
an open field in monticello at twelve
praying stitches in my belly would rip
you chased, embraced me you knew how fierce
the rage growing old like a war wound
growing old like newsprint I still see you
cutting gray hairs from
your skull like unwanted ghosts fixing yourself in
closet mirror for
another rendezvous. how my fists clench the seat when
you race down queens boulevard too radical for

the communist party and Dostoyevsky what power
you hide in your solitude a solitude I can only
watch from my own.
even now in death's deli you are my hero
a little old man who takes his
roast beef rare a woman discovering
her breasts.
we forget the cost of
living crawling into bed with
carbon copies and all these things
we continually bump against
in the dark.
it is not cold snow
that alarms
there is no going.
I am the one you chose
on a voyage inside yourself
where it is white and bilious
where even the dead laugh
where horses run and run against time
outside the angry illusion of
gravity and growing old in a body.
how to say what you have given me
the child behind your eyes.
you are my spiritual father
I chose you from the raw space
between worlds.
we are all growing old
in our new skin
to be born again
in each other.

White Light for Sally

for Sally Weisbord ("Aunt Sally")

"*Et lux in tenebris lucet*"
(*and the light shineth in darkness*)
from John I:1-5

Sally—you never got to dance at my wedding
& I never got to
eat those latkes you promised to make for me. standing at
santa monica pier I watch smog form over the ocean & think you'd see
diamonds not smog you'd see dignity not homeless
man angels not pizza boys you'd hear symphonies from
boom box. I stand at the pier while
you fight for life in long island hospital
now able to speak only with your eyes. I remember
you taking me by the hand, as a child, and showing me
where to find my strength—
something you never lost during
your twelve lymphoma years—never a complaint in
those awkward moments
a smile constant in
your voice as you ask "and how are you, dear."
you were right about everything even right about
my landlord
as I watch waves
crash against rocks I think I see you bending over in
the garden pruning roses your
oceanic blue eyes shiny as half
dollars. when I grow up
I want to be magnetic like you
like the time you took me to lunch in
your brown suede shoes from Italy the ones
surrounded by white light in my
closet shoes you wore when you picked me up

in little neck, snowstorm be damned, my tiny greek landlady
helping you downstairs you looked like a page out of a
five star hotel insisting we go to IHOP finding your escape from
great depression—from misguided belief
in mutual bonds and
mutual salvation from myths like reality and
collective renewal you knew, even then, survival is
a solitary affair the night you dropped me off my last
night in new york I held on to door of your cutlass supreme—
you got out and clung to door on the other side & we stood
in the snow crying our eyes out—a hard bargain to
survive, sometimes, we must walk away.
I never got to eat the latkes
you promised
paper rapidly replaces cutlery on table beside
hurricane lamp you gave me beside cobalt blue candles
where I renew myself like a nomadic vowel.
when I didn't have a computer you
had one built for me. Oh, we fought, too, like
the time in coffee shop that day I drove from
boston when you urged me to get teaching
credential—my drive back filled with rage—
you cared about me.
when you lay dying in hospital your sister came to beg
forgiveness—she didn't even have to ask—forgiveness
as natural to you as breathing as
that amazing man you married who sat me on his lap &
read to me from Dante his paradise still
inside you. there's a void where the void is there's
lightning on the shoes you gave me

storms be damned if we knew we invented everything
we'd never wake up.
Sally you never got to dance at my wedding why does life
have to break our hearts time &
time again in this war we wage from the front lines.
I salute you and
the grace you brought to
a sad lost planet.

to live with ghosts…

to live with ghosts
shed your skin
prepare to toss and
turn like light on a hurricane lamp
or a lover who lies in his sleep.
to live with ghosts
look for
the edge like
a pair of slippers that have
fallen apart like
your breath in
a soundproof room or the raw
wound of
a battered clock. to lie with ghosts
you must become a shadow
a futile campaign to awake to turn
without moving the lone particle of
dust that tells you where
the edge is.
to live with ghosts
you must prepare to die like one.

two pigeons

two pigeons perch on
the third rail watching for
a train they take turns pecking at
each other like newlyweds
their sweet caresses.
how did they get trapped on
the brink where
one movement left or right
might prove fatal
no matter the larger one flies off to
dance between the tracks—skipping gingerly
on metal links that urge
—nothing fearful here
he seems to say—
as I stand on the platform where
a train approaches————————oh my
oh my—moooove————————my scream echoes
in this vast, empty station
but long before the roar of
headlights the pigeon
nonplussed surges up
and back with uncommon
grace
to the space
where his lover by
the third rail waits.

at the end of rage

> *"Truly we are here
> on the roof of the world."*
> — J.M. Coetzee

Maybe a flight back east
will cure.
a sidewalk surrounds me like rain
it is night like a dumb beast
I want only future.
I watch as pain becomes a sneer
on the face of contempt.
city you are my mother
you are unfinished I am restless
it is not for me to judge
the city of my birth.
like a devout atheist
I am waiting to be disproved
on Elizabeth street a red ambulance struggles
like red brick your children little Italy
grown old with fear your women in designer
despair.
I hear the long solitary notes of a ripe flute
from a cracked tenement New York
you are my mother
though old and battered
your wisdom defies you
like an empty mirror in a crowded room
you remind us of our infirmity
like a nagging wife
you are an ancestor
in spite of yourself.
how I love your passion
Manhattan where survival is the ultimate revenge.

in San Francisco I speak broken Italian
with a lost sailor from Naples

where streetlights of hunger
hide men without roofs
from the sun.
a blind man sits outside an auto teller
on Montgomery street with his coin cup
he swears your gates are open
his cup is empty.
on Grant street fat chickens hang
in windows of Chinese merchants there is chatter
and fast feet.
I watch this city as the other
we are all cities waiting
to be watched.
at the end of rage
like a full beast
I must wander to stay awake
where are your vowels?
like a swollen nerve on a vital bed
there is no denying it—
there is no relief
but to stalk the streets
demanding only what is
alive and true.

far above the hills
we make love to ghosts we never knew
and awake with the taste
of sweat on our thighs.
O city where is your anger
asleep in the last car
of the last train out of penn station.

where is your anger
in a dumpsite collecting uranium
in sudden rifle of a lone lunatic
in macdonald's blitz in the terrible eyes
of a child on a bus O city
where is your anger?
we make love to ghosts
we never knew.
let the dead stay where they are
they will only go back to shadows
on the sheets ironic as the hot sun
on a cold hearse.
your ghosts walk
but they do not move strange city
your massive verves protruding
through a suit of ivory.
I am waiting to be disproved.
your ghosts walk
but they do not move.
give me back my rage O city
in uneven rhythms on drunken streets.
I will dance for you
red like a warrior
red with beginning.

even myths

1955
Googie's coffee shop
Sunset Blvd.
James Dean in
parking lot
legs strapped around
a motorcycle like a scene
from "the Wild One"
–just another poster boy
for posterity—fifty years later
James Dean
mounted on my wall
with the same
all knowing grin
wondering
would Narcissus be Narcissus
if not for the myth or just
another boy courting his
shadow in an
abandoned lake. this photo
of a myth pretending to be
another myth now poses as
November on my calendar—
if only I could reach across time—
tap him on the shoulder
& ask
what it's like to be captured like this
out of context is it
like dancing in a pool of standing water.
I might ask what he thinks
as the photographer adjusts
the lens
is he glad he wore

gloves are his pants too tight
is he hot in that Brando studded leather jacket
this contender
cigarette perched on
his parched lips looking like a child
at the circus
playing make-believe in a famous body
trying not to laugh or curse or
take the camera
too seriously
or himself
or that other fellow
who stares back
across time
Narcissus maybe or
Marlon Brando
while he straddles that bike thinking
someday someone somewhere will see him
and know even
myths have myths.

for Allen

for Allen Ginsberg

Saw an angel in the
elevator today he asked for
you—newspaper said
Allen Ginsberg dying—
newspapers lie.
a funny little rainbow forms
on microwave I write this
hoping it reaches
you take these words
roll them on your tongue
like lifesavers.
a large city you are wide
awake in the body
you have outgrown.
saw an angel in the
elevator he reminded me how
at sixteen I hung a
poster of you over my bed
only to have grandpa Moishe
exclaim "nice beard" how
at the "Y"
you shoved
an apple into
my mouth.
who did this to us
made us mortal
who did this
taught us to lie.
I write from your supermarket
in California
United Nations of misfits where fallen
entrepreneurs phenobarb their
way denying pain that is
consciousness while you sleep
with one eye open watching the best

minds of this generation prosaic
as prozac. who did this—
put savages in thousand dollar suits
and star
spangled gunmen
in capital
who killed the president
and didn't let him know
whose sad gnosis in
hot tub
Babylon.
a funny little rainbow forms
where you drop
surly articles proposing only
that which is preposterous
marriage of new spirit
in old jeans.
I see you
and your sane death in the cell you
carry around like a worn suitcase
frail and thin.
newspapers lie
now you are in Blake's
garden
rearranging anemones
waltzing with
Whitman
banging death on
Lorca's balcony.
who did this to us
put us in a body
who did this
who turned off the light.

The Russian Prince

for Bob Dylan

he was born when the lights went out
where investors in gold sold politicians
for Christ
where sweet music flows
hypnotic as Braille
and the truth inside is
twisted decimals above despair
he was born where fierce
tabloids launch from capes
of pure destiny.
kneeling at wailing walls
he was born when
the lights went out.

O minstrel boy in royal blue
voices of technologic poets explode
starry night dense with sound
as there is no going
but goes on.
infallible crosses of
Kiev carve small
circles for your eyes and butchers
of white Russia cannot betray you.
lone one wings
clipped by strange women alone
at last in
your home of poetry.

II.

he struggles for light
above smoke-
riddled mountains
winding in and out of
nightmares he summons oracular
white Russia to his
side she comes with
mute stench of Babi Yar her hair
braided and black
warning of slaughter
of wise children.
he wakes sideways
pouring his heart out
pitching his tent in doorways
of thunder.
he lifts his bow aims
where switch-
blades line trees and
nomads grind silver
into dust.
white Russia
in her long black veil
opens like a vowel.
the prince on fire
brings fruit and proverbs
she buries her head in his
hand he hides
in the long white shadow
the sun makes on the mountain.

III. The Minstrel's Song

deliver me
from traffic of
birth and death
from those who are always right.
deliver me
from another man's justice
from the truth if it is holy—
and those who prosper
from others' pain.
deliver me
from those who make slaves
of their sisters
and sell their brothers
into bondage
from those who bow down
to shadows on caves.
deliver me from doors that lock
from perjured piety
from judges and juries
from all those who trans-
form vision into pain.
I will do battle
with self-appointed angels
until I pass
through that wall of fire
and deliver those who cast
their cracked syllables
to the wind
abandon their chains for wings.

I will stand dumb before
the gate
like Moses and watch
the sea part from memory.
       deliver me
from those crippled with grief
who cling, like lepers,
to their skin of sorrow
and let me pass
       electric
through the light.

IV.

black magi on Macdougal street abandons
his mantra to a hooded beggar
unorthodox stars gather
to celebrate rainbows shoot like
halos overhead.

there is no home for the invisible
who learn the price of freedom
purging themselves on punitive
verbs of beginning.
he sings in a marketplace
with sudden explosion of Christ
Christ hanging from huge gold chains
around necks of Latino boys crucifixes
and prayer beads crushed in mouths of
small orphans.
it is for the exile to discover his shape

inside doorways vast and vacant
it is for women to turn to stone
it is for the priest who winds his
watch against dust tried and torn apart by
virgins history of inquisitions
and serenades where
Russia wide-hipped angular
Russia with blade in hand
Russia white-lined and furious hides.
the prince carves north star on a wall
turns back
his shadow dancing after him
down forbidding streets.

V.

hollow cheeks of his ancestors alarm
at first
rapid pulse blue light from
eyes he keeps hidden where lovers cling
magnetic with impulse
messengers arrive with cardboard signs.
he leaps from the landing
into gutter knowing
someone waits around the corner.
he is always looking at
the light the sun makes as
it sinks into the ground.
his head cocked like a rifle
ready to fire
he watches struggle of thieves

and angels stabbed by newspaper boys
while Antigone waits in the wings to
escape with the corpse.
foreigner among knives and
broken glass he witnesses another wedding
borne away on the back of a hearse.
his suitcase stuffed with forgetting
his back bent out of shape
like the little mining town where
he was born.
a sinister monk posing for reporters
he begs for space but
darkness is all and all
is darkness
and he is drawn,
again,
to the damp thighs of his birth,
brutally new.

(original version, June, 1977)

so we do the primitive

so we do the primitive
every time we turn
on the news
and make believe
it happens to
somebody
else
when it's
our ass
that's
getting cooked
along
with the rest of
them.

next door

bloated with
sleep
crawling out of
bed he
leaves
a scar on
the table
next to
the pen
that won't
write.
he wonders
why die
next door
to anything.

Execution Day in July

"Si muero,
dejad el balcon abierto."
— Garcia Lorca

despedida. farewell. gone
now
balcony barricaded from
oranges & wheat
you knew
too well
(the invisible still
moving about your
house in death-
defiance.)
despedida. farewell. gone
now
though bulldozers prey
on that ground your
soul-allotment
you rest
sterile to dirt,
like one of goya's
victims,
straighback
in almost enviable
detachment.

in faust's bed...

*(in climbing begins
the descent)*

for Philip Lamantia

The day melts
like a samurai on
his sword
what is said is already
spent
redundant as
a drifter's hand
where naked windows
collide in morning
we make a deal to
see. you climb
that blinding stairway where
erotic nightstands talk to
themselves of
criminal intent for
to see is
in days of dark
ever the highest crime as
what is whole
remains unknowable
the smile on
your face
in faust's bed
where we start
we finish
a terrible
wind at
our back.

you walk me

you walk me into
the eye of
the storm
without even
my gloves or
hat.
you teach me to
kneel where
fountains spring
oracular
could I subscribe
to the space
you leave
behind
I would
instead I'm obliged to
go another day
without you.

and sing your face

send for
me as you
would grace or
the last plate on
a furious table
send for me like
a quiet fire on
a crowded staircase or
a still life
dwarfed
by authentic
that we've
loved shows
only
that we
know no
better.
send for
me as day
sends for night
and I will
ride across the
globe in your
eyes and
sing your face.

walks large

I've got a
dream on
the tip of
my
tongue it's
so close I
can taste
it.
I've got
a name on
the back of
my spine
so close
I can hear it.
who says
it's easy
to fly
with
a clipped wing walks
large off
a stone
cliff.

heaven

that

to me

is

heaven

a blond

with

a

hairy

chest.

storm clouds

storm clouds

looming

overhead

somebody is

crying in

another

world.

But for the grace…

"That life is a suck and a sell, and nothing remains at the end but threadbare crepe and tears.

O camerado close! O you and me at last, and us two only."
— Walt Whitman

To whom do we owe the pleasure of freedom
To whom the duty of
dissent
To the children who stand on
milk cartons and watch
the cold rotting
rain or the battle
come home to
threadbare kitchens with
frank explosion on
a mother's
face as she buries
her only son in
small incestuous
towns where poets
stop to
witness the future
another sad rock in
death's suitcase.
To whom do we owe
the taste of sand on
a blade of grass
the subway or
a sudden bridge
those unseen
this hour
where still
we rejoice
inside
the pain.

the seasons

and so it's
winter here you
say as
you stammer
down the
stairs
can't you
tell by
the way the
birds hold
their breath
as they fall from
a blanket of
clouds where you
nest hugely like
daybreak on
the face of
a frozen lake.
and so it's spring
as you
show me
how to fly
as if
mortality is
nobody's business but
my own.
when we find ourselves
in record heat
still I reach
inside those parts of
you lean
from night like
a sparrow

filthy with rain and
carry your scent from
branch to
branch
all summer long.

fire escapes

why is it

I never connect

fire escapes

with fire

but

e

s

c

a

p

e

Convolutions

> *"That is God / A shout*
> *in the street."*
> —James Joyce

where angels come from
we have yet to discover
some say hell
some say los angeles.
on houston street
there is an angel born every
minute while a little grey
man fights with rats for
remains of frozen dinners.
it is hot
it is summer
a band of puerto rican boys shoot
footballs into baskets
a woman spreads in black mass
of torn wool on sidewalk—she has made this street
her bed.
crimes of passion are sold at newsstands
as sickness is a dream of health
abused by repetition.
I cross against the light
I can taste the sweat of construction workers
on tenement walls
the man next to me talks to himself
about death squads and eviction notices.
in close apartments we spawn intestate
buildings—buildings that expand
and contract like confiscated lungs.
on soto street a boy shows me his stripes
one for every life taken while he
stuffs plump strawberries
into his mouth little grey men

tango with gravity
where passion of otis redding
plays I hide
on bleecker streets behind
fresh vegetables thinking
who took the civil
out of civilization
waiting to cross where
angels come from
passion of otis
redding plays.

blue teeth

still-
born you
surrender in
urgent rain
taking parts of
me that grow hard in
your mouth and
swell between
your teeth urgent and
blue you
remember only
what disintegrates
and hammer me like
thunder
something fused
then forgotten I gush
inside
the storm.

The Bubblegum Thief

caught stealing bubblegum

of all crazy things! police

chased me down the road

one cop caught up to me & I

caught this stench his

voice

& he ask'd

"Are you the Sun?"

& I s'd

"No, but I've got good

connections!"

a bird

there's a

bird

chirping

outside

my

window

someone needs

to tell him

a storm is

coming.

interview with an angel

I asked an angel
how did you get so high
did you have to
climb on
top of
buildings?
he just shook
his head
will I need
my spiked
heels in
heaven?
no, he said,
just radial
tires
you'll find
torturers there, too,
who call themselves
saints.

their burgundy bloom

That's what
you call
an electric
wind on
the
balcony
where
roses stare
like frozen
geese and
the urgings
that
drive us
in their
burgundy
bloom
come &
go
like the naked
night.

hanging man

there is a man hanging at
the end of
a
tunnel
his hands
tied
behind
his back
a cord around
his throat
like
a figure
eight
how is it
the nastiest
places sound
lyrical like Abu Ghraib
where a guard
quietly counts
stones
then neatly folds
a sheet across
an iron crucifix. sooner or
later
war brings us all
to our knees
he thinks
war is
our alibi
when the void
no longer
works.

in translation

your blondeness at the top of the stairs
your blondeness parked
by a fragile red car
your blondeness
somehow eludes me.
it works for you like the vague hand
you open to close around mine
your chest alert with ancestral hair.
so much is lost in translation
in transition how I want to touch you
you'll disappear
into a Spain you have known and lost in boyhood
into your travel the impenetrable
universe the one you keep
locked in your head in the quiet
under the blondeness I cannot find a name for.
it is incurable this thirst
my tongue on your eyelids
your manliness in another language one that is foreign
but too familiar.
I wait at the bottom of the stairs
like a nocturnal cat sniffing for dawn
or is it danger I smell while you stand
awake in your blondeness vague
but not false.

USA donuts

open 24 hours!
USA donuts opposite
convenience market facing
chevron station
there is no doubt you are here
to serve full-
serve self-
serve there is no doubt
I am here munching stale
bran muffin while it rains perpetual while
it rains razorblades outside.
a comforting
thought this inside/outside how re-
assuring to think
that a simple piece of glass is
enough to separate.
some things freeze better
than others I think devouring
muffin like traffic and yes
it is all a movie your car telephones
and Nike ministries your starlets
and used car salesmen open 24 hours!
I watch as a palm reader hoarse from
too much sleep hustles an Asian guy
I watch your burned
burgers mysteriously trans-
form into turbo engines I watch
the manifest destiny of your parking lot
hungry in this world of credit cards
and gang shootings where everything
can be bought on time where even god
has an answering machine.
your sign proclaims open 24 hours

where the heart is just another
tank to fill with super
unleaded where the man with silver
hair hides behind windshield of his
BMW convinced he is invisible
and the trans-
lucent boy who is maybe a vision orders
a jelly donut with this Garbo-
like look in his eye
like maybe he has arrived
like maybe he does deserve to be here.

rain

I still smell you
in the morning
on my hands
rain against the roof
strong as
the bones of
your face
your hardness as deep
as hardness will go.
you are dark
in the light.
I still hear you
like thunder
I still feel you inside.

a fist of light

for Michael McClure

astonished as
glass shattered by
the roadside
I watch sleep
escape from you
raw as a lover
fresh from
the shower   you remember
the passing of
another like
a walk in
a dangerous
park or
fire in a foreign
tongue a substance
you have yet to
receive
your beauty
the makeshift
mattress from which
you descend
a room that is
nearly dark until you
enter
holding a fist of light.

PAST TENSE

for John Coetzee

He looked like the picture of raskolnikov on the cover of
crime & punishment penguin edition he talked like james
mason in lolita when he walked nerves would shoot out of
the soles of his shoes his undershirts were always stained
from his long walks home and no matter what he did with
his eyes they did not fit in their sockets.
sometimes I would watch him
it was like lifting the skin off the skull of
a corpse
and catching the wild veins as they shoot past.
what to do with the position of his nose?
the way he parts his smile is
particularly amusing
it is like the Red Sea splitting
historically.
Sometimes I would sit and watch
police cars shoot through his ears
he would bare his teeth like a wolf man
and I would know it was love.

courtroom chrysanthemum

I got caught
copping a
flower
from
the
    garden of Eden
&
two
saints
escorted me to
the
    local precinct
where
I
was
convicted of
trespassing
on
    celestial grounds.

it hurts, you say, to see

> *"What a bad joke the human heart is."*
> — *George Sand*

You wake
on the tip of
my tongue unauthorized
insert a scrambled
life then leave.
your pain becomes
a small fountain in
my throat
a past that looks on
without conviction.
you wrap around my bearded
chair dementia creeping up
like a war wound.
what battle is this
that winds too thin around you.
it hurts, you say, to see.

Prometheus

"Swollen bowels," he said
"that's all you get," then rose from hardwood
chair "I'm not a boy
anymore—no two ways
about it."
he reached into his pocket
producing a sound like
nerve gas
"the sun was half an hour late this
morning—a half hour late"
his tongue stuck to his lips as
he talked
he cracked knuckle after
knuckle in a
feeble attempt at unity.
he was contagious—
at least, he thought so.
I reached for a cigarette
he fumbled for his lighter with a grunt—
"when you eat fire
you gotta expect a little indigestion."
did he eat fire often, I asked
is that why his face stands away from his skull
like a frightened child.
what would he like for breakfast
what was it like being chained to a rock
does his liver hurt would he do it again.
"it wasn't for the fire,"
he said
"it was defiance."

The Still Point

"Except for the point, the still point,
There would be no dance, and there is only the dance."
— T.S. Eliot

Fireflies light up
the roof confused by
a moon that is
more or
less full. I am
irrefutably
alone while
waiting for
someone
who is stuck at
an airport.
the tiny bird
next door is
hoarse from
chirping in
an empty
house.
everything exists for conflict
even the dumb trail of
dust that climbs
the stairs
duped into
believing
the dance
survives all,
even us.

eating peanuts

eating peanuts and
writing a
poem I
think of
you
condemned now
to
memory.

Erogenous Zone

I want to feel your face in
the folds of my skirt as
your hand grips your fly.
I want to climb
the length of your
pants find sparks
your moan
electric as
morning.
I want to watch
your eyes new as
storms race
and roar
on
my thighs.

Playing Strip Poker with Tiresias

I claw my way into

the cage where he sits

a forgotten lion

waiting to

be tamed.

"What do you say,

old man—is there

room for

one more?"

"Pass the whiskey,

and my hat."

I do as he says,

and wait for daylight.

I have come a long

way to see

nothing.

Just the Same

I embrace you
under the skin
like fiction
before the fall
your face still warm
how quickly you tire of
angels and
merchants how quickly
you tire of
the street
where silence follows
you like a
sheet of rain
we walk among
shadows two soldiers lost to eternity.
just the same
I embrace you
under the skin.

(en francais)

Quand Meme

Je t'embrasse
sous la peau
comme la fiction
avant la chute
ton visage chaud encore
a quel rythme tu te lasses
des anges et

des marchands a quel rythme
tu te lasses
de la rue
ou le silence te suit
comme
un drap de pluie
nous marchons parmi
les ombres deux soldats perdus dans l'eternite.
quand même
je t'embrasse
sous la peau.

in a spirited debate

I sit in
a spirited
debate
with
the
sheets
while you
swear the
sun won't come up
without
you.

to dine with friends

I've got brecht on
the breakfast table
pound in the bread
crumbs proust in
the pantry dostoyevsky is
in with the knives while
mayakovsky recites from
the microwave.
I've got a garter full of
goethe faust in
with frosted flakes rimbaud in
the sink blake in
my stockings lorca
lingerie and
pockets full of poe   I find whitman in
with the washcloths
shelley with
the bone china   yeats
defiant as ever in his crystal vase and
rilke where only silverware
dares to go—O
to dine with friends
to dine on eternity.

Waking Up on the Wall Side

the coffee is burned
it smells like the E train
curtains sag—a pair of old breasts
hiding from the sun
and a slight fog descends upon
the maplewood circle where
I collect myself like dust on a vague epic.
there is something odious about sleep
it is so goddamned official.
waking up on the wall side
I reach for gravity
and a cigarette.
I look for the tiny dependable
clock on a chest I forgot to dust.
rolling over I reach
for a spark of light.

COMES LOVE

"Comes love nothing can be done."
for Artie Shaw

Words get in
the way of
what we want to
say to those we love
words push and shove
like prize fighters in
a toxic ring or
dreaded storms in
much-awaited spring
words can only sting
and bring us
closer to
the void where
language rules
among fools for
truth and silence
are next of kin
and those with
open mouths can only exchange
empty vows
but those whose music
is their heart
can never for too long
be apart
nor fear a darkness
that consumes
as flight
comes naturally to
we who
live to tell
who know
but cannot say
in the end
love has its way.

Le Monde N'Existe Pas Entre Nous

Le monde n'existe pas
entre nous
je te cherche dans
les rues de rilke
je te cherche dans
les rues fellinis
je te cherche dans
un grand
magazin
ou les enfants
jouent avec
le feu
comme un ange
sans eglise
un ange vrai
vraiment le monde
n'existe pas
entre nous.

The World Doesn't Exist Between Us

the world doesn't exist
between us
I look for you
on streets of rilke
I look for you
on streets fellini
I look for you
in a big
department store
where the children
are playing with
fire
like an angel
without a church
a real angel
really the world
doesn't
exist
between us.

Once

We were children once
before there was a wave
before thunder and
lightning
before highways and
hollow roads
before there was
a knowing
grin in
our back pockets.
We were children once
when magic
had a
middle name.

In Another Life

At some
point in
another life
we will
meet and
we will
kiss
again
as if
for
the
first
time.

Acknowledgments

The following poems have been published in the magazines, and anthologies, listed below:

"at the end of rage," *Exquisite Corpse*, Baton Rouge, Louisiana, 1986; *Stiffest of the Corpse* (edited by Andrei Codrescu), City Lights Books, San Francisco, California, 1989.

"For a soldier," *Poetry Magazine*, www.poetrymagazine.com, (online) autumn issue, 2003; *Poets Against the War*, online, 2003.

"The Russian Prince," *Poetry Magazine*, www.poetrymagazine.com, (online) winter, 2003-2004.

"elegy for democracy," Ibid.

"fire escapes," Ibid.

"in this city," Ibid.

"how it starts," Ibid.

"between the cracks," *Poetry Magazine*, www.poetrymagazine.com (online), winter issue, 2003-2004.

"Managing Gravity," *Lummox Journal*, July, 2003, Los Angeles.

"White Light for Sally," *Jack Magazine*, www.jackmagazine.com, June, 2003.

"On Waite Street," Ibid.

"in this city," www.amanoverboard.com, June, 2003.

"A Message from Jayne," *Beatitude 33: Silver Anniversary Issue*, May, 1985; also winner of Academy of American Poets Award, San Francisco, 1974.

"Walt Whitman's Fly," *Audit*, 1973, Buffalo, New York.

"The Crowning with Thorns," Ibid.

"Riding with Destiny," *Sic: Vice & Verse*, 2000, Los Angeles.

"For Allen," *Jack Magazine*, www.jackmagazine.com, 2001.

"Past Tense," *The New York Quarterly*, Issue 16, 1974, New York.

"No Small Accomplishment," *The New York Quarterly*, Issue 65, 2008, New York.

"Under That Bridge," *The New York Quarterly*, Issue 62, 2008, New York.

"Waking Up on the Wall Side," *The New York Quarterly*, Issue 29, 1986, New York.

"Playing Strip Poker with Prometheus" *Jack Magazine*, www.jackmagazine.com, 2010.

"The World Doesn't Exist Between Us," Ibid.

"U.S.A. Donuts," *The Jacaranda Review*, Vol. 4, No. 2, 1990, Los Angeles.

"For Jack," *Big Bridge*, online at: www.bigbridge.com, 2001.

"in translation," *City Lights Review*, No. 2, 1988, San Francisco.

"Execution Day in July," *Podium*, Vol. II, No. 2, 1969, Ohio.

"blind as Brooklyn," *Poetry Magazine* (online), and *Political Affairs Magazine*, 2005.

"an impulse like salt," *Poetry Magazine* (online), and www.the-hold.com, 2004.

"last time I looked," www.the-hold.com.

"When dark is put away," Ibid.

"Comes Love," Ibid.

"Convolutions," the-hold.com, March, 2004.

"to dine with friends" online at *The 3rd Page*, and *The Pedestal Magazine*, 2004.

"a special breed," *The Pedestal Magazine*, October, 2004.

"Passionata," *Last Call: The Legend of Charles Bukowski*, Lummox Press, 2004.

"a bird," *Jack Magazine*, www.jackmagazine.com, 2006.

"interview with an angel," Ibid.

"two pigeons," *Exterminating Angel*, online, 2006.

"a fist of light," *Ginosko Review*, Issue 4, 2007, San Francisco.

"But for the grace" online at www.the-hold.com 2005

"heaven," Ibid.

"and sing your face," Ibid.

"Erogenous Zone" online at www.the-hold.com, 2004.

"to be carried aboard," *Sic: Vice & Verse*, 2003, Los Angeles; *Oakland Out Loud*, 2007, a publication of PEN Oakland, 2007, Oakland.

"The Still Point," *The New York Quarterly*.

About the Author

Jayne Lyn Stahl has been publishing poetry since 1967. Her work has appeared in such notable magazines, and anthologies, as *The New York Quarterly, City Lights Review, Exquisite Corpse, Beatitudes: 33, Pulpsmith, The Jacaranda Review, Stiffest of the Corpse* (a City Lights publication), *Oakland Out Loud* (a publication of PEN Oakland), to name but a few, and been translated into Spanish, Italian, and French. Additionally, Ms. Stahl is a widely published essayist, *Huffington Post* blogger, as well as a playwright and screenwriter whose feature-length screenplay, "Shakespeare & Company," about the censorship battle to publish James Joyce's *Ulysses*, is currently in development. She is a member of PEN American Center, in New York, and PEN USA.

About NYQ Books™

NYQ Books™ was established in 2009 as an imprint of The New York Quarterly Foundation, Inc. Its mission is to augment the *New York Quarterly* poetry magazine by providing an additional venue for poets already published in the magazine. A lifelong dream of NYQ's founding editor, William Packard, NYQ Books™ has been made possible by both growing foundation support and new technology that was not available during William Packard's lifetime. We are proud to present these books to you and hope that you will continue to support The New York Quarterly Foundation, Inc. and our poets and that you will enjoy these other titles from NYQ Books™:

Joanna Crispi	*Soldier in the Grass*
Ira Joe Fisher	*Songs from an Earlier Century*
Ted Jonathan	*Bones and Jokes*
Fred Yannantuono	*A Boilermaker for the Lady*
Sanford Fraser	*Tourist*
Grace Zabriskie	*Poems*

Please visit our website for these and other titles:

www.nyqbooks.org

www.ingramcontent.com/pod-product-compliance
Lightning Source LLC
LaVergne TN
LVHW011426080426
835512LV00005B/296